GW00498512

Dick Turpin

by

THE AUTHOR:	Peter Norman Jackson
CO-WRITER AND RESEARCH:	Elaine Jackson
PHOTOGRAPHY:	Mark Antony Jackson
LOCATIONS AND MODEL:	Stephen Paul Jackson

ARTHUR H. STOCKWELL LTD.
Elms Court   Ilfracombe
Devon

ISBN 0 7223 2259-3

Printed in Great Britain by
Arthur H. Stockwell Ltd.
Elms Court   Ilfracombe
Devon

Acknowledgements

The Author wishes to thank all those here listed for their valuable assistance and co-operation throughout the research of this book:

Mr Glyn Williams, Landlord of The Rose & Crown Public House, Hempstead.

Epping Conservation Society, Information Centre.

Epping Library.

Mrs Langridge, 'Maskerade' Costume Hire, Sewards End, Saffron Walden.

Saffron Walden Library.

Cambridgeshire Libraries Collection.

The Folk Musuem, Cambridge.

Mrs Mitchell, Landlady of The Bull Hotel, Long Sutton.

York Castle Museum.

Author's Note

I am grateful to my daughter Elaine, and my two sons Stephen and Mark, for giving so much of their valuable time in helping with the research and photography to enable us to write this book.

Contents

List of Illustrations

Introduction

THE LIFE OF DICK TURPIN

Notorious Highwayman

This book sets out to trace the steps of Dick Turpin from 1706 until 1739 with facts and coloured illustrations as near as possible.

This book gives detailed information of the highlights of his life and the most important areas and places he frequented throughout his short life.

He stood five feet nine tall, of dark complexion, marked with smallpox, high cheek bones, upright and broad shouldered.

Gambling was one of his main attractions, and this appealed then as now, to all classes of society. He also loved the haunts of tipsters, thieves and rogues of every sort.

It was in such surroundings, that the following little romance, one of many, was staged.

12

One day in the Marylebone Gardens, a private estate, walked Mrs Fountayne the wife or sister-in-law of Dean Fountayne a pillar of established church, this lady was a noted beauty; Turpin had an eye for a beautiful woman.

This lady was taking in the sunshine when a well-dressed stranger strolled up to her, took the lady in his arms and kissed her most passionately on her lips. The lady struggled, Turpin raised his hat and said, ''Be not alarmed dear madam, you can now boast you have been kissed by Dick Turpin, good day madam.'' With that he strolled away and was lost in the crowd.

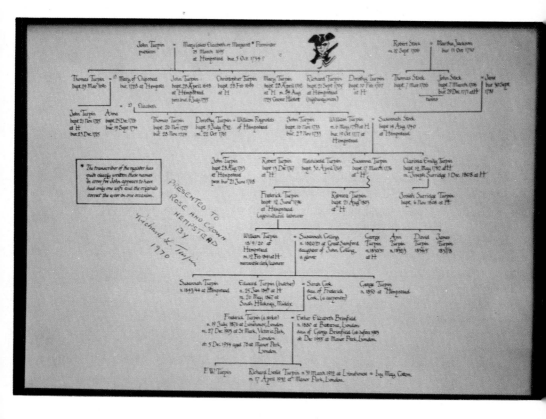

fig. 0

Chapter
1
Young Turpin

fig. 1

Dick Turpin was born in 1706 at Hempstead, near Saffron Walden in Essex. It is said that he was born at the alehouse now known as The Rose and Crown, however, I have certain information that this was not so. He was born in the small cottage in the village now known as The Old Post Cottage; he was still a baby in arms when his parents moved down the road to take up The Rose and Crown, then known as The Blue Bell.

The Old Post Cottage shown as it is today. (fig. 1.)

fig. 2

Turpin was raised in The Rose and Crown Public House, he spent
his childhood and early manhood there; the pub has changed very
little over the years, at one time a small section of the inn was used
as a butcher's shop.
(fig. 2.)

The public bar has changed little, there is still a wealth of old
beams and large open fireplace giving that olde worlde
atmosphere.
(fig. 3.)

There's still the old hook in the chimney breast (fig. 4) but the hole
in the ceiling through which Turpin would look down into the bar
from the bedroom above is sadly gone now.

fig. 3

fig. 4

In the end section of the pub, meat hooks can still be found along with the channel in the floor once used for washing down of the carcases. This section of the inn has now been opened up to form part of the public bar.

fig. 4a

The young Turpin was taught to read and write by a local teacher before taking up an apprenticeship in the butcher's shop in Thaxted, now known as Vincent Duckett's Ltd.
(fig. 5.)

He worked in the butcher's shop for some time before becoming restless; he then took up the notion to start up on his own, and so part of the inn, with his father's help, became a butchery. Turpin never made a go of his business as a butcher — he was always short of funds. So he took to going out at night and stealing cattle, slaughtering them and selling the meat in his shop; but this soon became rather dull for him and he soon wanted some other form of excitement.

At this time he acquired a cottage just across the road from his father's inn; the pretty little cottage with its thatched roof and exposed beams is today called 'Turpin's Cottage'. This is believed to have been three cottages at one time. Turpin soon set to work and built a slaughter house at the rear; rather a rough construction, but it served its purpose, for his midnight pursuits.
(fig. 6.)

He was always under suspicion with his meat dealings, but the village people had no complaints as to the prices of his meat. His family was well respected, and himself well liked for his stories and entertaining manner.

He was always about in the village and could be found in the inn most nights as he had a strong liking for ale; cock-fighting was common in Hempstead at this time, which always delighted Turpin, and he would join in for the fun. This barbaric game took place between a group of trees now known as 'Turpin's Ring', (fig. 7.) situated just across the road from the Rose and Crown Inn.

fig. 5

fig. 6

fig. 7

The main supply of water for the village was from the spring with its pumps; just opposite 'Turpin's Ring'. (fig. 8.)

The village of Hempstead in Turpin's childhood was full of life and activity, with the bakery and mill in full production and many cottage industries. The main street would have been full of farm labourers with horses and carts.

The old blacksmith's, sadly too, has been pulled down, with a new house built on the site, named 'Anvil-Rise' in memory of its past.

The pretty little stream was once a powerful river which drove the mill, and on many occasions flooded the village, cutting it off.

fig. 8

fig. 9

fig. 10

Turpin did go to church on a very few occasions; his family the Turpins and the Palmers (his mother's maiden name) are buried there, and Turpin was baptised there along with his brothers and sisters.

The church stands high, overlooking the village of Hempstead, and has changed very little over the years, apart from repairs and renovation works, and standing in its quite pretty churchyard one has to think that it would have been the perfect resting place for Turpin had his life turned in a different direction.
(fig. 9 & 10.)

Chapter 2
Highwayman

fig. 11

Illustration B. 21

Turpin took up the idea of robbing the rich, after all it was no hardship to them. He would set out after dark to Newport to await the stage-coach in London Lane.
(fig. 11.)

As the stage-coach came on its mad dash from Norwich to London, with its cargo of rich and famous, and as the coach slowed up to pass through the ford (fig. 12.), Turpin raised his gun and held up the coach with "Stand and Deliver".

He would rob them of their gold and jewellery, but he never hurt anyone. Then he would return to Hempstead before daylight; as time went by, this became a nightly pursuit.

fig. 12

fig. 13

Turpin always had an eye for a beauty and took his pleasures when he could, loving them and leaving them, until he fell in love with a beauty, one Betty Millington; and when Turpin became of age they were married. They took up residence in a quaint little cottage in Church Street, Thaxted.
(fig. 13 & 15.)

Now known as 'Turpin's Cottage', just across the road from the 'Cock Inn', where he would stable his horse to allow him to carry on with his nightly pursuits.
(fig. 14.)

With a little butchery in the day, when of course the 'Cock Inn' was not open — for when it was he could be found there drinking heavily, gambling and entertaining the traders that frequented the inn.

Little is known of Betty Millington; it is believed that she came from a well-respected family and was related to the teacher who taught Turpin to read and write; this may have been how they first came upon their acquaintance. She is known to have stood by Turpin through his drinking, gambling and highway robberies, trying to give the impression of leading a normal life within the community of Thaxted, giving him support and help with the disposal of jewellery from his nightly raids; this later on was to change, as life with Turpin gathered momentum.

fig. 14

fig. 15

Turpin's next little enterprise was to become the landlord of the 'Rose and Crown' Inn near Brook, otherwise known at that time as, Bull-Beggars-Hole at Clayhill.

With his wife installed in a cottage near by, Turpin spent his time gambling and entertaining the customers with his stories.

His tricks at this time for making money with very little or no work, was to rob the staying guests of their valuables while they slept soundly in their beds.

But only too soon this became dull and too easy for Turpin; there was no danger, no thrill and very little challenge for him. All the things he loved best and now missed.

As with so much of our countryside over the past years, great changes have taken place. Motorways have played their part in changing the face of our land, in some cases completely wiping out small villages and hamlets.

fig. 17

Turpin took his wife and moved next to Sewardstone, a small thatched cottage, one of four in Mott Street just a few steps down the lane from the 'Old Plough Inn', which was situated on the crossroads at Waltham Abbey to Chingford.

This row of small cottages has today been converted into one house, and is now called 'The Plough Cottage'.
(fig. 17.)

fig. 18

The Old Plough Inn, with its thatch roof and wealth of beams, got into such disrepair that sadly it had to be pulled down.

On the very same site today stands the new Plough Public House. (fig. 19.)

The whole area has changed greatly since Turpin's time, with nearly all the old cottages situated in a small community around the Plough Inn, now gone.

fig. 19

It was in their time living at Sewardstone, that Turpin started to hold-up and raid the stage-coaches as they made their way through Epping Forest; he would travel miles by night; no stage-coach was safe any more and travelling the road at this time became most hazardous.

One of his most daring hold-ups happened on the 6th June 1737; he held up the Saffron Walden and Bishop's Stortford stage-coaches as they were stopped at the very same spot, just outside Epping. He robbed both coaches, a most daring task. He was now carrying out numerous hold-ups, even in the daytime. Turpin was a master of his craft, he not only had to control his own horse but also keep his victims covered with his pistol while collecting anything of value from the coach and its passengers.

He was, there is no doubt, an outstanding horseman; he was so bold in his manner that very often he would ask the law directions to help him in his movements and the whereabouts of a stage-coach.

One of his favourite places to hold-up the coach was at the crossroads from High Beach to Epping.
(fig. 20.)

fig. 20

One of the stage-coaches can be seen on show at the York Castle Museum in all its splendour; just as it would have looked to Turpin. (fig. 21.)

fig. 21

Now Dick found family responsibilities appear more heavy with a wife and child to support, and shortly he found himself with piling debts as a result of extravagant living way beyond his means.

Having developed a taste for easy money he next turned his hand at house-breaking. It was at this time that a notorious band of thieves and robbers known as the Gregory's Gang had their headquarters in Epping Forest; this less dangerous and more profitable form of raids appealed to Turpin, so for the time being he gave up his stage-coach hold-ups and cattle rustling and took up with the Gregory Gang in Epping Forest and surrounding areas; the gang had a clearing in the forest where they would hold up after a night of raids on nearby farmhouses. (fig. 22.)

fig. 22

The Gregory's Gang consisted of seventeen men in all, and together they committed hundreds of robberies in Essex. There was Samuel Gregory, a blacksmith turned deerstealer. Thomas Rowden, who had been acquitted of counterfeiting. Jeremy Gregory, deerstealer and one time acquitted of shooting John Deakins. John Field, also a convicted deerstealer; along with Joseph Rose and John Fuller; not forgetting William Rogers. Mary Brazier, convicted of stealing and whipped, presumed to have met Joseph Rose in prison and became his companion. Herbert Haines, a barber and wig maker who one time had a shop in Hog Lane, Shoreditch. William Johnson, deerstealer and convicted murderer. West Drake companion of Herbert Haines; along with John Coster and John Gassey (alias Gaskey); and finally William Falconer, who turned king's evidence and went his own way.

Turpin, and his gang of no good desperados, carried out some brutal robberies, selecting lonely farmhouses for attack while the male occupants were away. Turpin and his mates tortured the occupants into yielding up valuables. A reward of fifty guineas was offered for each member of the gang.

On one occasion the gang went into a chandler's shop near the Loggerheads at Woodford Row, and called for a half pint of brandy. Soon they were joined by the rest of the gang; they had not been long in the shop when one of them pulled out a knife and then threatened the master of the house, his wife and daughter, with death. The rest rifled the house of everything of value. Two nights later a similar despicable event took place at Woodford. As the robberies became more numerous and violent, so the rewards were increased for any member of this notorious and much feared gang.

Illustration F. 23

Chapter
3
Tom King

Illustration D. 24

Turpin soon became tired of raiding farmhouses with the Gregory Gang and took up his old pastime once more of highwayman. On this occasion as he was awaiting the stage-coach, a young man on a bay chestnut drew his pistol at Dick demanding that he surrender his valuables. Dick laughed aloud "Have you not heard of honour among thieves or in our case among highwaymen"; and so it was that Tom King and Dick Turpin entered into a partnership and became more like brothers than just companions. (fig. 23.) And so they rode together throughout Epping Forest and the main road to London taking all they could get from the stage-coaches. Together they dug a cave hidden by fern and brambles on the eastern side of the forest on the high road between Kings Oak and Loughton. The cave being large enough to hold the two bandits and their horses. On many occasions when they were held up there, Dick's wife Elizabeth would bring them clean clothes and fresh food. (fig. 24.)

fig. 23

fig. 24

Robbing the stage-coaches, Turpin and King never had any difficulties in disposing of the stolen goods, such as rings, watches and pearls; anything of value they would take.

Their chief ally was the landlord of the Red Lion near Hatton Garden, who hid his criminal activities as a 'fence', being one of the most notorious in London at that time, by running an alehouse as his cover.

Turpin would call at the Red Lion to dispose of their ill-gotten gains. On occasions when this was not possible, due to the fact that by now Turpin was the most wanted man in England with a reward of two hundred guineas for his delivery, Turpin's wife Elizabeth would make the trip to the Red Lion on his behalf.

Turpin and King took the clever precaution of shoeing their horses with circular shoes so as to give no indication as to which way they made their escape.

Unfortunately due to vast re-development in the Whitechapel and Hatton Garden area, the Red Lion has been lost and made way for new enterprises.

Illustration AA. 1

The time Turpin rode with Tom King, nicknamed 'Swift-nix' by Turpin, was one of the happiest times in his life; but events were to take a turn that would soon destroy that.

One Thomas Morris, a servant of the keeper Thompson of Epping Forest, set out to trap Turpin in his cave. When he came upon Turpin, Turpin took up his loaded pistol and shot Morris dead. It was the first time throughout Turpin's misdemeanours that he had to shoot anyone.

On the next occasion Turpin stole a fine black horse from a Mr Major near the Green Man in Epping Forest. Turpin took a shine to this beautiful animal and kept the beast for his own personal use.

Word had it that Turpin and King could be found at the Red Lion in Whitechapel. The constable came across Tom King on the road and was on the point of arresting him for the theft of this fine horse when Turpin rode up.

fig. 25

King shouted to Turpin to take up his piece and shoot the constable. This incident took place on the site then known as 'Fairmead' at the crossroads to London from High Beach and Loughton, one of their favourite places to hold-up the stage-coach.

Now there's a roundabout, and on the site of this tragic incident nearby, stands the 'Robin Hood' public house. (fig. 25.)

At this moment the London bound stage-coach appeared; Turpin's horse reared up and Turpin's pistol fired, but it did not strike down the constable as first intended, instead he accidentally shot Tom King. Turpin took flight into the forest, he was deep in remorse for the death of his best friend, and could never forget or forgive himself for what had happened, let alone ride their favourite haunts.

The area where this took place, and King died, has changed a great deal over the years, but there is a feeling about the area, it seems to have left its mark; it certainly did as far as Turpin goes, for what took place that day started a new chain of events in Turpin's life.

fig. 26

Now Turpin was wanted for just about every felony there was in the book. A large gang of men and constables with tracker dogs set out to take Turpin dead or alive.

But Turpin was always just one jump ahead of the law, and while he made his escape on his faithful horse 'Black Bess' northward, his pursuers were still combing the forest.

fig. 26a

fig. 28

Turpin held up in Cambridge to rest himself and Black Bess at the small inn on the crossroads of Castle Street.

fig. 27

Today this is called 'The Folks Museum', its interior is quaint and little has changed; it's full of interesting items regarding Cambridge in its early years. As for the exterior it has undergone many renovations. (fig. 27.)

He next moved further up the hill of Castle Street to stay at the 'Three Tunns Inn' notorious for its vagabonds and thieves where he would be in more familiar company. Sadly the 'Three Tunns Inn' had to be pulled down, but a drawing shows how the inn would have looked shortly before its demolition took place. (fig. 28.)

Turpin could never stay anywhere long if he was to keep one step ahead of the law. Cambridge at this time was teaming with excisemen.

And he soon had another narrow escape from the peace officers. He had left his bedroom in the 'Three Tunns Inn' for the stable yard to attend to his horse's needs, when the officers arrived.

Dressed as he was in very little, he immediately mounted Black Bess and rode off, leaving behind his belongings; a hat, coat, doublet, mask, cravat, spurs and even his pistol.

Later, the then landlord displayed the items to his customers describing how they had been left behind by none other than the most notorious highwayman Dick Turpin.

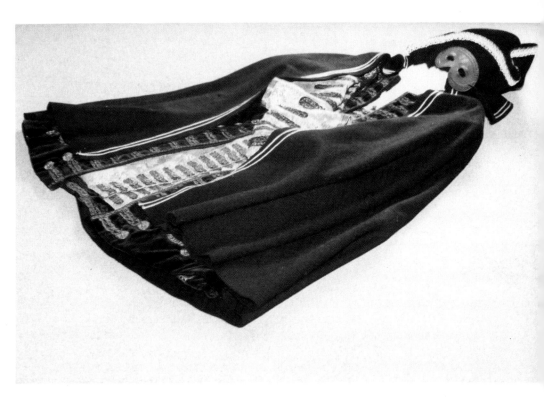

fig. 29

fig. 29a

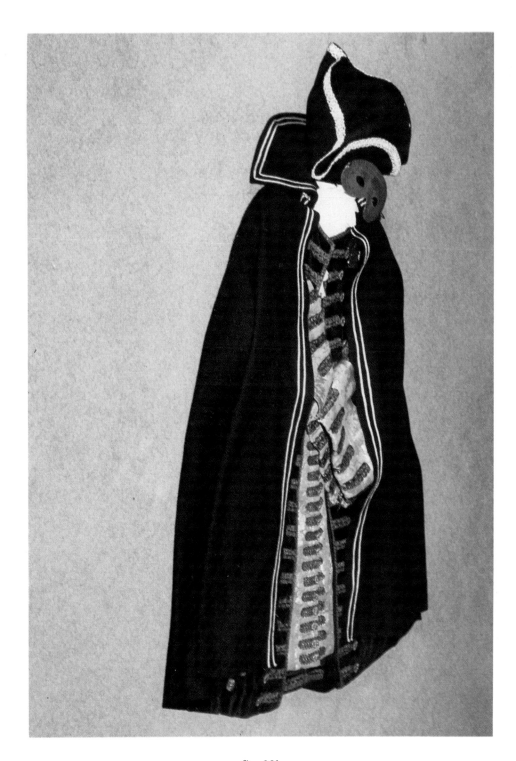

fig. 29b

Chapter 4
Yorkshire

fig. 30

Turpin decided to move on, every hold-up became more dangerous, since he could never tell whether the next stage-coach would be a decoy.

With his mind made up on Lincolnshire, he set out in easy stages stopping only for one night at inns along the way; many pubs and inns boast having had Dick stay there; but with him moving on so quickly there is little, if any proof, so as to state which ones were honoured with his presence.

fig. 31

He found his next safe haven at Long Sutton; here he was unknown and able to introduce himself under an assumed name, that of Richard Palmer a horse dealer, (Palmer being his mother's maiden name).

Turpin made his home at 'The Bull Hotel', renting rooms there and trading as a horse dealer, with horses that he stole from farms on nightly raids.

He soon became well liked, and a respected citizen having been accepted in Long Sutton, and entertained frequently in the Bull Hotel.
(fig. 30.) (fig. 31.)

The Bull Hotel at Long Sutton was built around four hundred years ago, minor alterations have been carried out over the years to the interior, but it has kept its olde worlde charm; and a visit takes one back in time.
(fig. 33.) (fig. 34.)

The exterior of the property has been renovated with a red-brick front. But in Turpin's time it was constructed of lath and plaster as is shown by a picture hanging in the bar.
(fig. 32.)

The hotel was a central meeting place for local traders, and the old auction sale-room can still be found on the first floor.

fig. 32

fig. 33

fig. 34

It was at this time in Long Sutton that he returned to visit his family at the inn of his childhood back in Hempstead.

Turpin's family were the only people with whom he could be himself, who despite the crimes of robbery and murder would not betray him to the authorities for the reward they might obtain. This is not to say his actions were condoned by them, merely that despite what he was, he was nonetheless John Turpin's son, who had brought them disgrace; but they were a close family and would suffer all this to keep Dick from being sent to his death.

They may not have understood him or even how he had become the most wanted man in England, but the ties were still recognised and his visits were always something of an occasion, when despite considerable risk he came back to the place of his birth and upbringing.

It was on this occasion that Dick brought along a horse as a gift for his father, and together with his own horse they were stabled together at the inn. The stables are still there today and are virtually as they would have been on his visit.
(fig. 35.) (fig. 36.) & (fig. 37.)

fig. 37

fig. 36

fig. 35

Unknown to John Turpin, the horse received as a gift had been stolen; and at a later date after Dick had returned again to Long Sutton, a constable came inquiring as to where John Turpin had obtained the animal. John Turpin now found himself charged with stealing the horse, and as he refused to reveal how he had obtained it, he was duly arrested and incarcerated in Chelmsford.

Dick learned of his father's fate through an address to which he could be reached in Yorkshire if ever the need arose. And about this time he was to learn that he was the last surviving member of the Gregory Gang, and this must have finally brought home to him the absolute futility of his own position.

Illustration C. 20

fig. 38

Life had been going well in Long Sutton until a complaint of sheep stealing was lodged against him. Mr Delamere the local Justice of the Peace issued a warrant for his arrest. The warrant was served by a constable, but Turpin knocked him down and made his escape.

As door after door now closed on him, it was time to move on with the law close on his heels. So Turpin left Long Sutton and headed north once more, travelling by night through well-covered countryside, he drove on pushing himself and his horse to the limits until finally his faithful friend and companion Black Bess collapsed and died.

Turpin now stole a mount to complete his journey from farms along the way, taking a fresh horse, leaving behind the tired one.

He crossed the Humber River by boat one evening and landed at Brough, here he rented rooms at The Ferry Inn and gave his name as Richard Palmer once again.
(fig. 38.)

He soon made himself familiar with the local areas, introducing himself as a dealer of fine horses.

fig. 39

Turpin, found nearby Welton to his liking, and quickly established himself there; for apart from his great knowledge of cock-fighting and other sports, he was also an excellent judge of cattle and horses; his opinions were welcomingly accepted.(fig. 39.)

He was generally a man's man; for his love of sport, gambling and not forgetting his drinking, all these activities he soon took up again with relish. He was free and prospering; he also had enormous luck at the races, winning large sums of money. There seemed to be no shadow of suspicion as to his real identity and life seemed very enjoyable once again. But a black cloud was appearing on Turpin's horizon.

Dick became concerned about his father John Turpin who was detained in Chelmsford Gaol for Dick's wrongdoing. With word coming of his father's failing health, and his mother now at rest in Hempstead churchyard, Dick's sister Dorothy Rivernall and his brother-in-law were managing the inn (then known as The Blue Bell).

Surely now Turpin could see the man he had become; he was responsible for his own dear father being detained in such an awful place. But no, he was still unable to do the honourable thing and give himself up. Instead he remained at Welton wallowing in self-pity; it was a state he remained in for some time until at last in desperation of news he wrote to his brother-in-law for word; but his brother-in-law refused to except the letter saying he had no correspondent in Yorkshire.

He very often went out hunting and shooting with several gentlemen farmers in the neighbourhood, and was known to call often on one gentleman farmer who had a pretty daughter.

All seem to be well until that dreadful day outside The Cock Inn, when an event took place that was to change Turpin's life dramatically this time.

Sadly as with so many old thatched inns, The Cock Inn has been pulled down, but it stood in its hey-day next to the Old Jail House. (fig. 40.)

fig. 40

Turpin was returning from a day's shooting, when he saw one of the landlord's cockerels in the street, out in front of the Old Jail House. He shot and killed it. Mr Hall, his neighbour, seeing him shoot this cockerel said to him "Mr Palmer you have done wrong", where upon Turpin (Palmer) replied, if he would only stay while he recharged his piece he would shoot him too.

Mr Hall, horrified at being threatened, went at once and told the landlord of what had just taken place. On hearing this the landlord went with Mr Hall to see Mr George Cowle and obtained a warrant for apprehending Palmer (Turpin).

Upon this, Turpin was then taken to the general quarter sessions held at Beverley; he was escorted by Carey Gill and rode upon a gelding; he made no attempt to escape which was completely out of character for him. This notorious villian still clung to his anonymity, and rode with the constable to Beverley; here was a highwayman coming to the end of his road. On arriving late they rented a room at the then called Blue Bell Inn.

The Blue Bell Inn was virtually destroyed by fire and was rebuilt in 1794 and is today known as The Beverley Arms Hotel. (fig. 41.)

fig. 41

fig. 42

The next morning, on arrival at the court house, Turpin was questioned by George Cowle, Hugh Bethel and Marmaduke Constable, all three of his majesty's Justices of the Peace for East Riding of Yorkshire.

These three men demanded sureties for his good behaviour, and Palmer (Turpin) refused to supply them; so he was taken to the house of correction, in Register Square, now The Guild Hall.

Turpin now, for the very first time, found himself behind bars. He was held while investigations were carried out as to his identity.

The Guild Hall has undergone two major renovations and alterations since Turpin was held there.
(fig. 42.)

Shooting the fowl was a piece of bloody-mindedness, probably brought on by an unsuccessful morning's shooting, which had aggravated his already volatile mood.

It was an irresponsible act, which undoubtedly was the beginning of his downfall.

Illustration E. 17

Chapter 5
York Castle Prison

fig. 43

Mr Cowle realized this was very unusual that not one person could be found to stand surety for Palmer, and the fact that no one knew of his business affairs or where he had come from before settling in the district.

Mr Cowle decided further afield inquiries were called for. He had demanded to know from Palmer (Turpin) where he had lived and the nature of his business before coming to Welton. Turpin told him he had lived in Long Sutton and was a butcher by trade, with mounting debts he had been forced to move north.

The magistrate was not satisfied and sent Mr Appleton to Long Sutton to make inquiries as to the truth. Mr Appleton returned with a very different story, that Palmer was wanted for sheep and horse stealing and assaulting a constable. In fact he had no family residing there, and no one knew where he had come from, before he took up rooms at The Bull Hotel. This was confirmation for the Clerk of Peace, that Palmer was not who he claimed to be, and that he should be moved to York Castle. (fig. 43.)

With Palmer (Turpin) now safely installed in York Castle Prison, every effort was made to discover his past history. It soon became clear that his horse-trading was with stolen animals; there was sufficient evidence to commit him for trial.

74

York Castle is now a museum; the very cell where Turpin was locked up in 'death's row' is now open to the public.(fig. 44.)

fig. 44

The big heavy door closed behind Turpin; his freedom had come to an end. All he could see of the outside world was through the bars in the tiny cell window. (fig. 45.)

The accommodation in the cell was very basic; stone sink with cold water; wooden-slatted bed; very cold and damp. (fig. 46 & 47.)

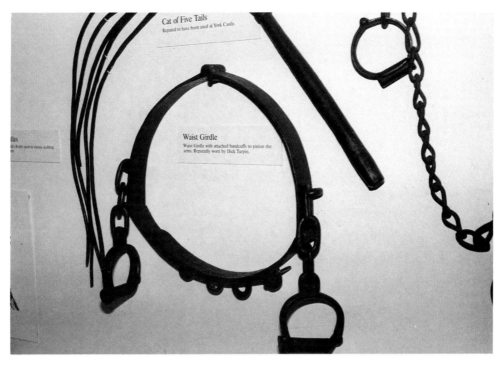

Cat of Five Tails
Reputed to have been used at York Castle.

Waist Girdle
Waist Girdle with attached handcuffs to pinion the arms. Reputedly worn by Dick Turpin.

fig. 45

fig. 45a

fig. 46

fig. 47

Instead of preparing his defence against the charges now brought, Turpin indulged himself with visitors; wagers were freely offered as to his conviction.

Although this was allowed, he was locked in leg irons during all such visits. These irons are on show in the cell. (fig. 48.)

fig. 48

Illustration A. 20

Chapter 6
The Trial & Execution

Turpin now made his next mistake — which this time would turn out to be his last. Although he should have realized the dangerous situation he was now in and give no further clues as to his real identity, he took up his pen and wrote a letter to his family, informing them of his confinement in York Castle Prison for horse stealing, and his need of surety, but still keeping the concealment of his real identity, and asking them not to neglect his plea.

But all was not well; with his father still in Chelmsford Prison and his brother-in-law still resident at the inn in Hempstead, Dick's letter refused by Pomp Rivernall, was returned to the post office with the postage unpaid.

Mr Smith a teacher, who infact had taught Dick to read and write just happened to be in the post office and saw the letter returned. He immediately recognised the handwriting of his former pupil. Paying for the postmark, he then set off to York Castle Prison where he felt sure he could identify the prisoner as Richard Turpin. On his arrival and explanation, the prisoners held were paraded before him; he had no difficulty in picking out Turpin.

Turpin's spirits must have now been distraught for his real identity was now proclaimed, and caused quite a sensation. The daily papers were full of the news that Turpin, the most notorious highwayman, was at last going to be brought to justice.

With the news of Turpin, now leading headlines, many witnesses were to come forward as to Turpin's wrongdoings, and slowly the case was prepared for the Grand Jury.

John Turpin was now released from prison; his good behaviour while there, and the pending trial of his son, all taken into consideration, he was set free.

The trial of Richard Turpin, alias Palmer, took place at York Assizes on March 22nd 1739 before Hon. Sir William Chapple. The jury of twelve men were; William Calvert, Samuel Waddington, William Popplewell, John Lambert, Robert Wiggen, William Wase, Thomas Simpson, George Smeaton, Robert Thompson, William Frank, James Boyes and Thomas Clarke.

Never before had a trial taken everyone's interests; the lower classes took him to their hearts for a loser who had put up one hell of a fight.

Country folk flocked to see him, taking him wine and other luxuries.

Turpin said very little as he stood in the dock; he asked for his trial to be moved to Essex, to give him time to prepare his defence and bring forth witnesses as to his character.

His request was denied and the jury brought a verdict of guilty; the Hon. Sir William Chapple sentenced him to death by hanging.

Surely now Dick was resigned to his fate; he received a letter from his father expressing his great grief at his son now under sentence of death, and sending his undying love with his hope that his son would be received in the eternal kingdom of God.

The date of execution was set for Saturday 7th April 1739.

Like an actor not wanting to disappoint his public, he prepared himself, purchasing a new frock coat and new shoes.

He showed no sign of weakness or remorse and spent his last few days boasting of his adventures and drinking with his many visitors.

The condemned cell is now called Pompey's Parlour, and there is a plate on the wall in Turpin's memory.
(fig. 49.)

York. April 10. Last Saturday Richard Turpin and John Stead were executed here for Horse stealing. The latter died very penitent, but the former behaved with the greatest Assurance to the last. It was remarkable, that as he mounted the Ladder, his Right Leg trembled, on which he stampt it, with an Air and undaunted Courage look'd round about him, and after speaking a few Words to the Topsman, he threw himself off the Ladder, and expired in about five Minutes; before his Death he declar'd himself to be the notorious Highwayman, Richard Turpin, and confess'd to the Topsman a great Number of Robberies which he had committed.

fig. 49

Now Turpin's time had come and he was prepared to make his exit. Dressed in his new clothes he mounted the cart which was followed by five mourners, each paid £3.10s. by Dick for their services.

A vast crowd had gathered just outside the town wall where the gallows stood. Turpin showed no sign of fear, and with great courage he chose the moment of his own end.

With undaunted courage, he declared himself to the onlooking crowd to be the notorious highwayman Richard Turpin. Apart from the slaughter of Tom King, for which he expressed deep regret, he confessed to one other murder.

He bequeathed his personal property to his family; but a gold ring, to a woman of beauty, with whom he was acquainted in Brough. He also acknowledged his wife and his child.

Then without waiting for the cart to move off, he flung himself from the ladder and expired instantly.

Illustration AB. 1

Turpin had played his final scene; his body was brought back from the gallows and placed at the Blue Boar at Castle Gate. The next morning he was buried in a coffin in St. George's Churchyard.

Sadly St. George's Church has been pulled down, but the tiny churchyard remains with Turpin's grave and headstone taking pride of place. (fig. 50.)

fig. 50

Two days later several persons were discovered removing his body from the grave. The mob having got word of this and suspecting it was to be anatomised, went to a garden in which the body was deposited and took Turpin's body triumphantly through the streets and buried it in the same grave; first having covered it with lime to prevent it being anatomised.

And so Dick Turpin the popular hero was finally laid to rest.

fig. 51

fig. 52

The
End